Great

First

Lines

D0827343

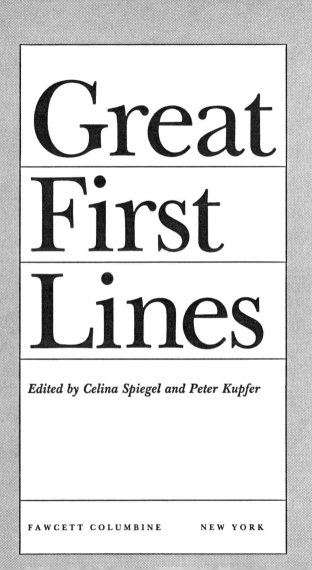

Great First Lines

Edited by Celina Spiegel and Peter Kupfer

FAWCETT COLUMBINE   NEW YORK

A Fawcett Columbine Book
Published by Ballantine Books

Foreword and Compilation copyright © 1992 by
Celina Spiegel and Peter Kupfer

Library of Congress Catalog Card Number: 91-78405

ISBN: 0-449-90772-8

Cover and text design by Beth Tondreau Design

Manufactured in the United States of America
First Edition: May 1992
10   9   8   7   6   5   4   3   2   1

for Donne and Bertrand

Foreword

"It was love at first sight." (44)

In any love affair, a first encounter can play a decisive role. When we open a book, the first sentence either entices us to read on or leaves us with little desire to become better acquainted.

Of course, initial impressions are sometimes misleading. A promising beginning does not always herald a masterpiece, just as many works of great literature have unremarkable beginnings. (Who can recall the opening of *Madame Bovary*?) A great first line, though, can contain the germ of an entire novel.

And so we offer you 200 "great first lines"—and leave you to guess the novels they introduce. (Answers are in the back.)

Most are from classics; a few are not, but we found them irresistible. Some will appear as familiar as old friends, others, more arcane, may be identified by style or subject.

While collecting these lines, we discovered that many began in similar ways, and a few were conscious parodies or references; when placed together, they created new resonances, or even humor. They tell a story of their own, and we hope their sequence will lend additional pleasure to the quotes themselves. Most of all, we hope that these lines will inspire you, as they inspired us, to return to your bookshelves to read, or re-read, the great novels from which they are taken.

C.M.S.
P.K.

Great

First

Lines

nce upon a time and a very good time it was there was a moocow coming down along the road and this moocow that was coming down along the road met a nicens little boy named baby tuckoo. . . .

It was the best of times, it was the worst of times, it was the age of wisdom, it was the age of foolishness, it was the epoch of belief, it was the epoch of incredulity, it was the season of Light, it was the season of Darkness, it was the spring of hope, it was the winter of despair, we had everything before us, we had nothing before us, we were all going direct to Heaven, we were all going direct the other way—in short, the period was so far like the present period, that some of its noisiest authorities insisted on its being received, for good or for evil, in the superlative degree of comparison only.

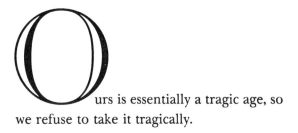

Ours is essentially a tragic age, so we refuse to take it tragically.

I wish either my father or my mother, or indeed both of them, as they were in duty both equally bound to it, had minded what they were about when they begot me; had they duly considered how much depended upon what they were then doing;—that not only the production of a rational Being was concerned in it, but that possibly the happy formation and temperature of his body, perhaps his genius and the very cast of his mind;—and, for aught they knew to the contrary, even the fortunes of his whole house might take their turn from the humours and dispositions which were then uppermost:—Had they duly weighted and considered all this, and proceeded accordingly,—I am verily persuaded I should have made a quite different figure in the world, from that, in which the reader is likely to see me.

ustoms of courtship vary greatly in different times and places, but the way the thing happens to be done here and now seems the only natural way to do it.

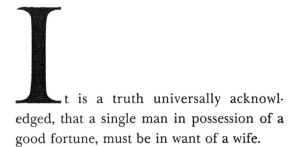

It is a truth universally acknowledged, that a single man in possession of a good fortune, must be in want of a wife.

was ever of opinion that the honest man who married and brought up a large family did more service than he who continued single, and only talked of population.

In the ancient city of London, on a certain autumn day in the second quarter of the sixteenth century, a boy was born to a poor family of the name of Canty, who did not want him.

"Where's Papa going with that ax?" said Fern to her mother as they were setting the table for breakfast.

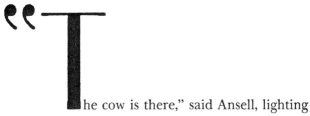

"The cow is there," said Ansell, lighting
a match and holding it out over the carpet.

"And—and—what comes next?"

 was born in the year 1632, in the city of *York*, of a good Family, tho' not of that Country, my Father being a Foreigner, of *Bremen*, who settled first at *Hull*: he got a good Estate by Merchandise, and leaving off his Trade, lived afterward at *York*, from whence he had married my Mother, whose Relations were named *Robinson*, a very good Family in that Country and from whom I was called *Robinson Kreutznaer*; but by the usual corruption of words in *England*, we are now called, nay we call ourselves, and write our Name *Crusoe*; and so my Companions always call'd me.

By the time he was nineteen Vance Weston had graduated from the College of Euphoria, Illinois, where his parents then lived, had spent a week in Chicago, invented a new religion, and edited for a few months a college magazine called *Getting There*, to which he had contributed several love poems and a series of iconoclastic essays.

hether I shall turn out to be the hero of my own life, or whether that station will be held by anybody else, these pages must show.

f you really want to hear about it, the first thing you'll probably want to know is where I was born, and what my lousy childhood was like, and how my parents were occupied and all before they had me, and all that David Copperfield kind of crap, but I don't feel like going into it, if you want to know the truth.

Happy families are all alike; every unhappy family is unhappy in its own way.

ll happy families are more or less dissimilar; all unhappy ones are more or less alike," says a great Russian writer in the beginning of a famous novel (*Anna Arkadievitch Karenina*, transfigured into English by R. G. Stonelower, Mount Tabor Ltd., 1880).

The idea of eternal return is a mysterious one, and Nietzsche has often perplexed other philosophers with it: to think that everything recurs as we once experienced it, and that the recurrence itself recurs ad infinitum!

I have been here before," I said; I had been there before; first with Sebastian more than twenty years ago on a cloudless day in June, when the ditches were white with fool'sparsley and meadowsweet and the air heavy with all the scents of summer; it was a day of peculiar splendour, such as our climate affords once or twice a year, when leaf and flower and bird and sun-lit stone and shadow seem all to proclaim the glory of God; and though I had been there so often, in so many moods, it was to that first visit that my heart returned on this, my latest.

*r*iverun, past Eve and Adam's from swerve of share to bend of bay, brings us by a commodius vicus of recirculation back to Howth Castle and Environs.

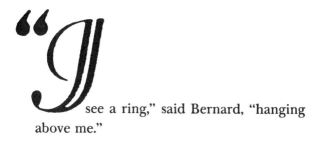

"**I** see a ring," said Bernard, "hanging above me."

o be born again,' sang Gibreel Farishta tumbling from the heavens, 'first you have to die.'

So, then people do come here in order to live; I would sooner have thought one died here.

shall soon be
quite dead
at last
in spite
of all.

Once you have given up the ghost, everything follows with dead certainty, even in the midst of chaos.

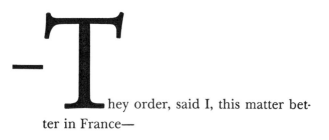

hey order, said I, this matter better in France—

I stand at the window of this great house in the south of France as night falls, the night which is leading me to the most terrible morning of my life.

In certain provincial towns there are houses whose appearance arouses a melancholy as great as that of the gloomiest cloisters, the most desolate moorland, or the saddest ruins.

he story had held us, round the fire, sufficiently breathless, but except the obvious remark that it was gruesome, as on Christmas Eve in an old house a strange tale should essentially be, I remember no comment uttered till somebody happened to note it as the only case he had met in which such a visitation had fallen on a child.

ne evening of late summer, before the 19th century had reached one-third of its span, a young man and woman, the latter carrying a child, were approaching the large village of Weydon-Priors, in Upper Wessex, on foot.

n easterly is the most disagreeable wind in Lyme Bay—Lyme Bay being that largest bite from the underside of England's outstretched southwestern leg—and a person of curiosity could at once have deduced several strong probabilities about the pair who began to walk down the quay at Lyme Regis, the small but ancient eponym of the inbite, one incisively sharp and blustery morning in the late March of 1867.

Saturday afternoon in November was approaching the time of twilight, and the vast tract of unenclosed wild known as Egdon Heath embrowned itself moment by moment.

ow in these dread latter days of the old violent beloved U.S.A. and of the Christ-forgetting Christ-haunted death-dealing Western world I came to myself in a grove of young pines and the question came to me: has it happened at last?

As I walked through the wilderness of this world, I lighted on a certain place, where there was a den; and I laid me down in that place to sleep: and as I slept I dreamed a dream.

or a long time I used to go to bed early.

ast night I dreamt I went to Manderley again.

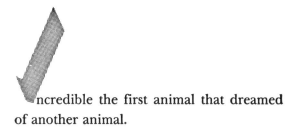ncredible the first animal that dreamed
of another animal.

hen Gregor Samsa woke up one morning from unsettling dreams, he found himself changed in his bed into a monstrous vermin.

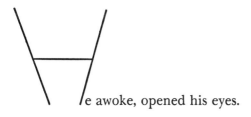e awoke, opened his eyes.

*H*erman Broder turned over and opened one eye.

When the fair gold morning of April stirred Mary Hawley awake, she turned over to her husband and saw him, little fingers pulling a frog mouth at her.

I think I fell in love with Sally while she was eating breakfast, the first time we were together.

ften he thought: My life did not begin until I knew her.

t was love at first sight.

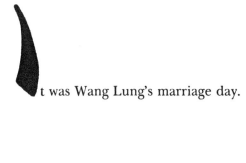t was Wang Lung's marriage day.

t was inevitable: the scent of bitter almonds always reminded him of the fate of unrequited love.

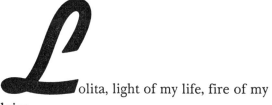

Lolita, light of my life, fire of my
loins.

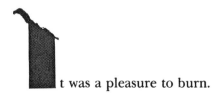t was a pleasure to burn.

oow-ow-ooow-owow!

uck did not read the newspapers, or he would have known that trouble was brewing, not alone for himself, but for every tide-water dog, strong of muscle and with warm, long hair, from Puget Sound to San Diego.

tately, plump Buck Mulligan came from the stairhead, bearing a bowl of lather on which a mirror and a razor lay crossed.

here is Edward Bear, coming downstairs now, bump, bump, bump, on the back of his head, behind Christopher Robin.

*A*ll children, except one, grow up.

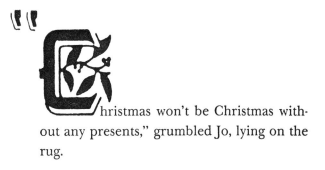

"Christmas won't be Christmas without any presents," grumbled Jo, lying on the rug.

ou don't know about me without you have read a book by the name of *The Adventures of Tom Sawyer*; but that ain't no matter.

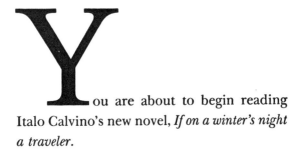

You are about to begin reading Italo Calvino's new novel, *If on a winter's night a traveler.*

I have never begun a novel with more misgiving.

Dr. Weiss, at forty, knew that her life had been ruined by literature.

Shortly after dawn, or what would have been dawn in a normal sky, Mr. Artur Sammler with his bushy eye took in the books and papers of his West Side bedroom and suspected strongly that they were the wrong books, the wrong papers.

"You've been reading the wrong books," the businessman said.

Alice was begin-
ning to get very tired of sitting by her sister
on the bank and of having nothing to do:
once or twice she had peeped into the book
her sister was reading, but it had no pictures
or conversations in it, "and what is the use
of a book," thought Alice, "without pictures
or conversations?"

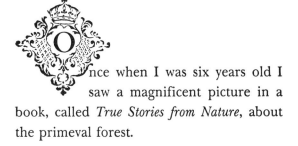nce when I was six years old I saw a magnificent picture in a book, called *True Stories from Nature*, about the primeval forest.

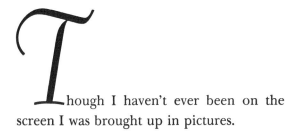

hough I haven't ever been on the screen I was brought up in pictures.

**F**or many years I claimed I could re-
member things seen at the time of my own
birth.

, Tiberius Claudius Drusus Nero Germanicus This-that-and-the-other (for I shall **not** trouble you yet with all **my** titles) who was once, and not so long ago either, known to my friends and relatives and associates as "Claudius the Idiot", or "That Claudius", or "Claudius the Stammerer", or "Clau-Clau-Claudius" or at best as "Poor Uncle Claudius", am now about to write this strange history of my life; starting from my earliest childhood and continuing year by year until I reach the fateful point of change where, some eight years ago, at the age of fifty-one, I suddenly found myself caught in what I may call the "golden predicament" from which I have never since become disentangled.

ppollon Appollonovich Ableu-khov was of venerable stock: he had Adam as his ancestor.

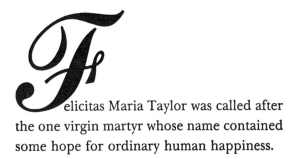elicitas Maria Taylor was called after
the one virgin martyr whose name contained
some hope for ordinary human happiness.

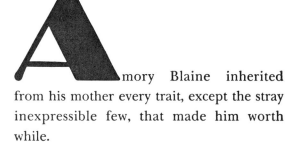Amory Blaine inherited from his mother every trait, except the stray inexpressible few, that made him worth while.

y father's family name being Pir-
rip, and my Christian name Philip, my infant
tongue could make of both names nothing
longer or more explicit than Pip.

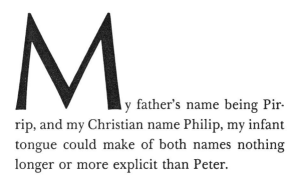

y father's name being Pir-
rip, and my Christian name Philip, my infant
tongue could make of both names nothing
longer or more explicit than Peter.

Call me Ishmael.

all me, Ishmael.

all me Jonah.

I am an American, Chicago born—Chicago, that somber city—and go at things as I have taught myself, freestyle, and will make the record in my own way: first to knock, first admitted; sometimes an innocent knock, sometimes a not so innocent.

t the beginning of the summer I had lunch with my father, the gangster, who was in town for the weekend to transact some of his vague business.

In my younger and more vulnerable years my father gave me some advice that I've been turning over in my mind ever since.

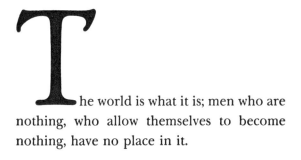

The world is what it is; men who are nothing, who allow themselves to become nothing, have no place in it.

Someone must have traduced Joseph K., for without having done anything wrong he was arrested one fine morning.

Mr. Jones, of the Manor Farm, had locked the hen-houses for the night, but was too drunk to remember to shut the popholes.

he door opened to reveal an infinitely spacious room: a whole world of meanings and motivations, not just a limited space buried in a mass of detail.

he cell door slammed behind Rubashov.

get the willies when I see closed doors.

ranted: I am an inmate of a mental hospital; my keeper is watching me, he never lets me out of his sight; there's a peephole in the door, and my keeper's eye is the shade of brown that can never see through a blue-eyed type like me.

I am an invisible man.

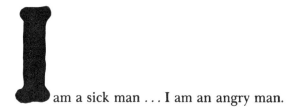I am a sick man ... I am an angry man.

rude thoughts and fierce forces are my state.

In eighteenth-century France there lived a man who was one of the most gifted and abominable personages in an era that knew no lack of gifted and abominable personages.

n author ought to consider himself, not as a gentleman who gives a private or eleemosynary treat, but rather as one who keeps a public ordinary, at which all persons are welcome for their money.

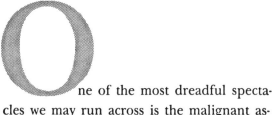

One of the most dreadful spectacles we may run across is the malignant aspect of a certain class of the Parisian populace; a class horrible to behold, pallid, yellow, tawny.

hate the faces of peasants.

In the days when the spinning wheels hummed busily in the farmhouses—and even great ladies, clothed in silk and thread lace, had their toy spinning wheels of polished oak—there might be seen, in districts far away among the lanes, or deep in the bosom of the hills, certain pallid undersized men who, by the side of the brawny country folk, looked like the remnants of a disinherited race.

While the present century was in its teens, and on one sunshiny morning in June, there drove up to the great iron gate of Miss Pinkerton's academy for young ladies, on Chiswick Mall, a large family coach, with two fat horses in blazing harness, driven by a fat coachman in a three-cornered hat and wig, at the rate of four miles an hour.

he past is a foreign country: they do things differently there.

It is three hundred forty-eight years, six months, and nineteen days ago today that the citizens of Paris were awakened by the pealing of all the bells in the triple precincts of the City, the University, and the Town.

In a certain corner of la Mancha, the name of which I do not choose to remember, there lately lived one of those country gentlemen, who adorn their halls with a rusty lance and worm-eaten target, and ride forth on the skeleton of a horse, to course with a sort of starved greyhound.

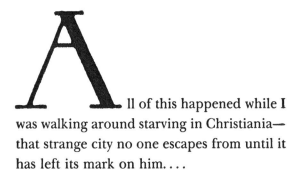

All of this happened while **I** was walking around starving in Christiania—that strange city no one escapes from until it has left its mark on him. . . .

am not mad, only old.

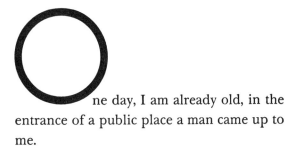ne day, I am already old, in the entrance of a public place a man came up to me.

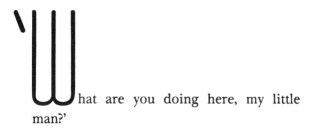'hat are you doing here, my little
man?'

Y ou are not the kind of guy who would be at a place like this at this time of the morning.

I can feel the heat closing in, feel them out there making their moves, setting up their devil doll stool pigeons, crooing over my spoon and dropper **I** throw away at Washington Square Station, vault a turnstile and two flights down the iron stairs, catch an uptown A train ... Young, good looking, crew cut, Ivy League, advertising exec type fruit holds the door back for me.

When Caroline Meeber boarded the afternoon train for Chicago, her total outfit consisted of a small trunk, a cheap imitation alligator-skin satchel, a small lunch in a paper box, and a yellow leather snap purse, containing her ticket, a scrap of paper with her sister's address in Van Buren Street, and four dollars in money.

Roy Hobbs pawed at the glass before thinking to prick a match with his thumbnail and hold the spurting flame in his cupped palm close to the lower berth window, but by then he had figured it was a tunnel they were passing through and was no longer surprised at the bright sight of himself holding a yellow light over his head, peering back in.

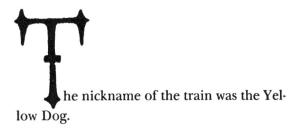The nickname of the train was the Yellow Dog.

first heard of Ántonia on what seemed to me an interminable journey across the great midland plain of North America.

To the red country and part of the gray country of Oklahoma, the last rains came gently, and they did not cut the scarred earth.

sharp clip-clop of iron-shod hoofs deadened and died away, and clouds of yellow dust drifted from under the cottonwoods out over the sage.

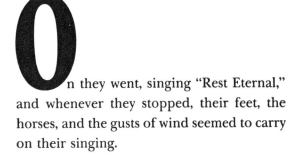

On they went, singing "Rest Eternal," and whenever they stopped, their feet, the horses, and the gusts of wind seemed to carry on their singing.

We are at rest five miles behind the front.

he cold passed reluctantly from the earth, and the retiring fogs revealed an army stretched out on the hills, resting.

t was a feature peculiar to the Colonial wars of North America, that the toils and dangers of the wilderness were to be encountered, before the adverse hosts could meet.

n army post in peacetime is a dull place.

At ten o'clock the poker players around the sitting-room table were beginning to nod over their game.

he huge black clock hand is still at rest but is on the point of making its once-a-minute gesture; that resilient jolt will set a whole world in motion.

t was a bright cold day in April, and the clocks were striking thirteen.

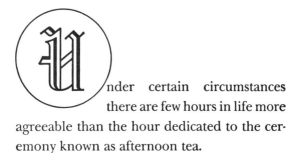nder certain circumstances there are few hours in life more agreeable than the hour dedicated to the ceremony known as afternoon tea.

ne summer afternoon Mrs. Oedipa Maas came home from a Tupperware party whose hostess had put perhaps too much Kirsch in the fondue to find that she, Oedipa, had been named executor, or she supposed executrix, of the estate of one Pierce Inverarity, a California real estate mogul who had once lost two million dollars in his spare time but still had assets numerous and tangled enough to make the job of sorting it all out more than honorary.

From a little after two oclock until almost sundown of the long still hot weary dead September afternoon they sat in what Miss Coldfield still called the office because her father had called it that—a dim hot airless room with the blinds all closed and fastened for forty-three summers because when she was a girl someone had believed that light and moving air carried heat and that dark was always cooler, and which (as the sun shone fuller and fuller on that side of the house) became latticed with yellow slashes full of dust motes which Quentin thought of as being flecks of the dead old dried paint itself blown inward from the scaling blinds as wind might have blown them.

ur eyes register
the light of dead stars.

screaming comes across the sky.

throng of bearded men, in sad-colored garments and gray, steeple-crowned hats, intermixed with women, some wearing hoods, and others bareheaded, was assembled in front of a wooden edifice, the door of which was heavily timbered with oak, and studded with iron spikes.

y true name is so well known in the records or registers at Newgate, and in the Old Bailey, and there are some things of such consequence still depending there, relating to my particular conduct, that it is not to be expected I should set my name or the account of my family to this work; perhaps, after my death, it may be better known; at present it would not be proper, no, not though a general pardon should be issued, even without exceptions and reserve of persons or crimes.

It is a trite but true observation that examples work more forcibly on the mind than precepts, and if this be just in what is odious and blameable, it is more strongly so in what is amiable and praise-worthy.

he Mole had been working very hard all the morning, spring-cleaning his little home.

he day had gone by just as days go by.

he sun shone, having no alternative,
on the nothing new.

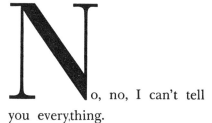o, no, I can't tell
you every,thing.

ou tell.

He—for there could be no doubt of his sex, though the fashion of the time did something to disguise it—was in the act of slicing at the head of a Moor which swung from the rafters.

Weidmann appeared before you in a five o'clock edition, his head swathed in white bands, a nun and yet a wounded pilot fallen into the rye one September day like the day when the world came to know the name of Our Lady of the Flowers.

adinho, Dona Flor's first husband, died one Sunday of Carnival, in the morning, when dressed up like a Bahian woman, he was dancing the samba, with the greatest enthusiasm, in the Dois de Julho Square, not far from his house.

**S**omething a little strange, that's what you notice, that she's not a woman like all the others.

The tradesmen of Bridgepoint learned to dread the sound of "Miss Mathilda," for with that name the good Anna always conquered.

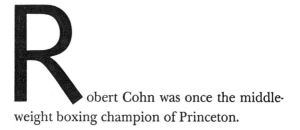obert Cohn was once the middle-
weight boxing champion of Princeton.

e was an inch, perhaps two, under six feet, powerfully built, and he advanced straight at you with a slight stoop of the shoulders, head forward, and a fixed from-under stare which made you think of a charging bull.

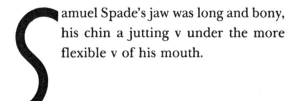

amuel Spade's jaw was long and bony, his chin a jutting v under the more flexible v of his mouth.

he damn'd blood burst, first through his nostrils, then pounded through the veins in his neck, the scarlet torrent exploded through his mouth, it reached his eyes and blinded him, and brought Arthur down, down, down, down, down.

here were crimson roses on the bench; they looked like slashes of blood.

he bench on which Dobbs was sitting was not so good.

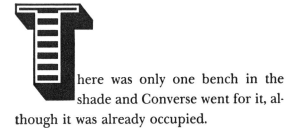here was only one bench in the shade and Converse went for it, although it was already occupied.

Through the fence, between the curling flower spaces, I could see them hitting.

The boys, as they talked to the girls from Marcia Blaine School, stood on the far side of their bicycles holding the handlebars, which established a protective fence of bicycle between the sexes, and the impression that at any moment the boys were likely to be away.

I went back to the Devon School not long ago, and found it looking oddly newer than when I was a student there fifteen years before.

Though brilliantly sunny, Saturday morning was overcoat weather again, not just topcoat weather, as it had been all week and as everyone had hoped it would stay for the big weekend—the weekend of the Yale game.

It was dolphin weather, when I sailed into Piraeus with my comrades of the Cretan bull ring.

*T*he boy with fair hair lowered him-self down the last few feet of rock and began to pick his way toward the lagoon.

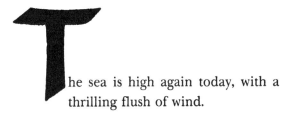

The sea is high again today, with a thrilling flush of wind.

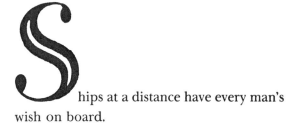

Ships at a distance have every man's wish on board.

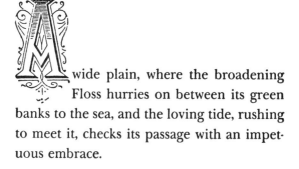A wide plain, where the broadening Floss hurries on between its green banks to the sea, and the loving tide, rushing to meet it, checks its passage with an impetuous embrace.

e was an old man who fished alone in a skiff in the Gulf Stream and he had gone eighty-four days now without taking a fish.

The *Nellie*, a cruising yawl, swung to her anchor without a flutter of the sails, and was at rest.

One January day, thirty years ago, the little town of Hanover, anchored on a windy Nebraska tableland, was trying not to be blown away.

*O*n a cold blowy February day a woman is boarding the ten a.m. flight to London, followed by an invisible dog.

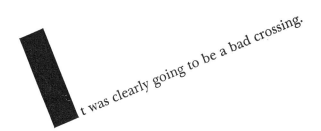

It was clearly going to be a bad crossing.

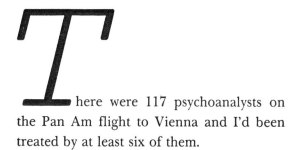

here were 117 psychoanalysts on the Pan Am flight to Vienna and I'd been treated by at least six of them.

*T*here was a depression over the Atlantic.

his is the saddest story I have ever heard.

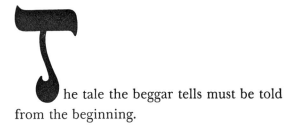he tale the beggar tells must be told
from the beginning.

t might be most dramatically effective to begin the tale at the moment when Arnold Baffin rang me up and said, "Bradley, could you come round here please, I think that I have just killed my wife."

My dear friends, I knew you were faithful.

I have noticed that when someone asks for you on the telephone and, finding you out, leaves a message begging you to call him up the moment you come in, as it's important, the matter is more often important to him than to you.

had the story, bit by bit, from various people, and, as generally happens in such cases, each time it was a different story.

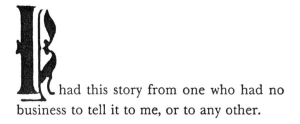had this story from one who had no business to tell it to me, or to any other.

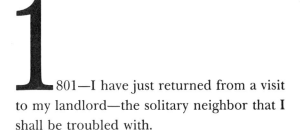

1801—I have just returned from a visit to my landlord—the solitary neighbor that I shall be troubled with.

"I see ..." said the vampire thoughtfully, and slowly he walked across the room towards the window.

Mr. Utterson the lawyer was a man of a rugged countenance that was never lighted by a smile; cold, scanty and embarrassed in discourse; backward in sentiment; lean, long, dusty, dreary and yet somehow loveable.

There lived in Westphalia, in the castle of the Baron of Thunder-Ten-Tronckh, a young man on whom nature had bestowed the perfection of gentle manners.

n a hole in the ground there lived a hobbit.

green hunting cap squeezed the top of the fleshy balloon of a head.

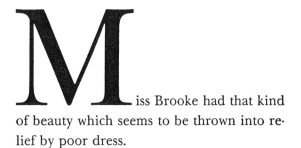

Miss Brooke had that kind of beauty which seems to be thrown into relief by poor dress.

carlett O'Hara was not beautiful, but men seldom realized it when caught by her charm as the Tarleton twins were.

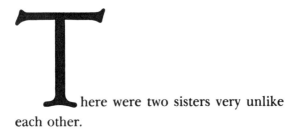

There were two sisters very unlike each other.

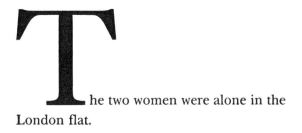

The two women were alone in the London flat.

Here we are, alone again.

In the town there were two mutes, and they were always together.

You better not never tell nobody but God.

am writing this because people I love
have died.

other died today.

y first act on entering this world was to kill my mother.

She was so deeply imbedded in my consciousness that for the first year of school I seem to have believed that each of my teachers was my mother in disguise.

or a short while during the year I was ten, I thought only people I did not know died.

What can you say about a twenty-five year-old girl who died?

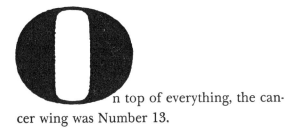n top of everything, the cancer wing was Number 13.

arley was dead, to begin with.

ied on me finally.

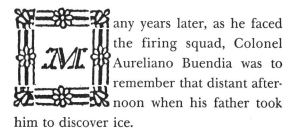any years later, as he faced the firing squad, Colonel Aureliano Buendia was to remember that distant afternoon when his father took him to discover ice.

nd so they've killed our Ferdinand, said the charwoman to Mr. Svejk, who had left military service years before, after having been finally certified by an army medical board as an imbecile, and now lived by selling dogs—ugly, mongrel, monstrosities whose pedigrees he forged.

Riding up the winding road of Saint Agnes Cemetery in the back of the rattling old truck, Francis Phelan became aware that the dead, even more than the living, settled down in neighborhoods.

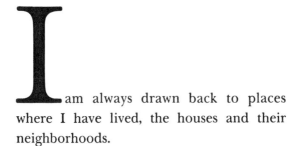

I am always drawn back to places where I have lived, the houses and their neighborhoods.

alf-way down a by-street of one of our New England towns, stands a rusty wooden house, with seven acutely peaked gables facing towards various points of the compass, and a huge, clustered chimney in the midst.

The towers of Zenith aspired above the morning mist; austere towers of steel and cement and limestone, sturdy as cliffs and delicate as silver rods.

Asquat grey building of only thirty-four stories.

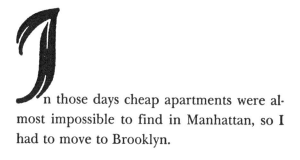

n those days cheap apartments were almost impossible to find in Manhattan, so I had to move to Brooklyn.

*S*erene was a word you could put to Brooklyn, New York.

It was a queer, sultry summer, the summer they electrocuted the Rosenbergs, and I didn't know what I was doing in New York.

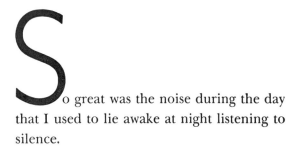

So great was the noise during the day that I used to lie awake at night listening to silence.

obody could sleep.

'What's it going to be then, eh?'

There was a time when people were in the habit of addressing themselves frequently and felt no shame at making a record of their inward transactions.

The cabin-passenger wrote in his diary a parody of Descartes: "I feel discomfort, therefore I am alive," then sat pen in hand with no more to record.

Answers

1. James Joyce, *A Portrait of the Artist as a Young Man*, 1916
2. Charles Dickens, *A Tale of Two Cities*, 1859
3. D.H. Lawrence, *Lady Chatterly's Lover*, 1928
4. Laurence Sterne, *The Life and Opinions of Tristram Shandy*, 1767
5. Herman Wouk, *Marjorie Morningstar*, 1955
6. Jane Austen, *Pride and Prejudice*, 1813
7. Oliver Goldsmith, *The Vicar of Wakefield*, 1766
8. Mark Twain, *The Prince and the Pauper*, 1882
9. E.B. White, *Charlotte's Web*, 1952
10. E.M. Forster, *The Longest Journey*, 1907
11. Thomas Mann, *Buddenbrooks* (tr. H.T. Lowe-Porter), 1902
12. Daniel Defoe, *Robinson Crusoe*, 1719

13. Edith Wharton, *Hudson River Bracketed*, 1929

14. Charles Dickens, *David Copperfield*, 1850

15. J.D. Salinger, *The Catcher in the Rye*, 1951

16. Leo Tolstoy, *Anna Karenina* (tr. Constance Garnett), 1877

17. Vladimir Nabokov, *Ada, or Ardor: A Family Chronicle*, 1969

18. Milan Kundera, *The Unbearable Lightness of Being* (tr. Michael Henry Heim), 1984

19. Evelyn Waugh, *Brideshead Revisited*, 1945

20. James Joyce, *Finnegans Wake*, 1939

21. Virginia Woolf, *The Waves*, 1931

22. Salman Rushdie, *The Satanic Verses*, 1988

23. Rainer Maria Rilke, *The Notebooks of Malte Laurids Brigge* (tr. M.D. Herter Norton), 1910

24. Samuel Beckett, *Malone Dies*, 1951; Beckett's English version, 1958

25. Henry Miller, *Tropic of Capricorn*, 1939

26. Laurence Sterne, *A Sentimental Journey*, 1768

27. James Baldwin, *Giovanni's Room*, 1956

Index of Authors

Index of Titles

Acknowledgments

"I had the story bit by bit, from various people, and, as generally happens in such cases, each time it was a different story." (162)

Indeed, we owe thanks to "various people" for suggesting their own favorite first lines. We are grateful for the contributions of Alan Andres, Christina Büchmann, Jeanne Heifetz, Peter Morris, Maggie Elliott, Jonathan Rosen, and Eugene Stein; for the bookshelves of Dan Dubno, Minna Elias, Debbie Hautzig, Dara Lurie, Aaron and Helen Spiegel, Shari Spiegel, and Mychal Springer; to Shakespeare & Co., Endicott Books, Barnes & Nobles, and the New York Public Library, St. Agnes Branch. Special thanks to John Herman and Alan Andres for their early encouragement, and to Mary South and Cindy Klein for their enthusiasm and for helping us see the project through. Most of all we are grateful to Donne Pinsky and Bertrand Denieul, to whom this book is dedicated.